Two-Face God

Two-Face God

Poems by Jason McCall

WordTech Editions

Published by WordTech Editions
P.O. Box 541106
Cincinnati, OH 45254-1106

ISBN: 9781625492524

Poetry Editor: Kevin Walzer
Business Editor: Lori Jareo

Acknowledgements

Thankful acknowledgement is given to the following journals in which the poems listed below first appeared:

Archaeopteryx: "Janus Bifrons" and "Janus Works the Door"
Banango Street: "Apology to Montgomery" and "Montgomery, 1998"
Cartridge Lit: "When I Heard Another White Woman at the Bar Talking About Michael Vick and the Death Penalty" and "When Your *Madden* Running Back Retires"
Cream City Review: "Thanksgiving"
Hieroglyph: "If All the Masters of Time Were My Slaves" and "Medea's High School Reunion"
Los Angeles Review: "Friday the 13th"
Marsh Hawk Review: "Now That Wally West Is Black" and "Trayvon's High School Reunion"
Poetry is Dead: "The Time God"
Rappahannock Review: "January," "Wally West at the End of Time," and "We Love Throwback Thursday"
Rattle: "Roll Call for Michael Brown"
Specter Magazine: "Remix"
Sundog Lit: "Hacking," "Home Games," and "Never Have I Ever"

"Remix" was also published in the chapbook *Mother, Less Child* (Paper Nautilus, 2014)

Table of Contents

The Time God

Let the other gods swing their hammers and brag
about unbreakable shields,

infallible spears, and Omega Beams.
He only needs a chair

to show you his power. Sit down
next to a pretty face at happy hour

and pay your tab with a knife
wound and a beat up baby

picture in your wallet.
Sit down and watch the game.

Watch your world go from *I want*
to be like that guy to *I know that*

guy to *I could have been, yeah,*
I could have been that guy.

Sit down after a day in the world,
sit down and measure

his power by how many times
your bones swear,

how many times you pray
for one more hour in the day.

Montgomery, 1998

Because this is Montgomery in 1998,
the first lessons I learn in 7th grade are I can't
say nigger too loud and all students need
to wear t-shirts under their Barkley jerseys.

Because this is Montgomery in 1998,
I'm smart enough not to say nigger
too loud so my parents send me away
to the gifted school downtown.

Because this is Montgomery in 1998,
"gifted" means mostly white
kids who can't fight
or can't afford private school.

Because this is Montgomery in 1998,
my white friend in Latin won't talk to me
about anything other than No Limit Records
and *East Bay* books.

Because this is Montgomery in 1998,
Most of my dreams end with a light-skinned girl's legs
in English class. One or two dreams
will never leave the Latina who gave me my only nickname.

Because this is Montgomery in 1998,
the school year really doesn't matter
because no one notices me stringing up
my Terrell Davis cross trainers on the first day.

Because this is Montgomery in 1998,
my grandmother dies
and I feel weak when I try to hold up
my fainting mom in church.

Because this is Montgomery in 1998,
my biggest failures are my failure to dunk
and my failure to raise
my eyebrow like The Rock.

Because this is Montgomery in 1998,
I'm the last kid at home, waiting for the hum
of a car in the driveway while I count all the ghosts
I want to be when I grow up.

Wally West at the End of Time

Speed kills
memory. Does lightning

mourn the rent oak?
Does the viper's jaw lament

the hare's lost milestones?
How long did I run

to get back to the apartment before blood
stained the carpet? How many times

have I circled the world
to find myself naked

in the mirror after my first time?
Only the past holds

promise. How many
footprints have you left

on your grandchildren's grave?
Have you ever watched your failures swell

until all earths are pock-scarred and sore?
Every future is a bullet

with seven billion names.
Where are the watchtowers

and guardians? The end is neither Atlantean
throne nor apocalyptic fire pit.

It belongs to the phantom
snails and the star-nosed moles.

Don’t lose the sun.
Don’t lose the sun.

My First Day of School

I left with lip stick on my collar
and my mother hit me when I came home
with questions about marriage
and mixed babies
and my 5-year-old brain
didn't know how to do much
other than blush and shrug.
I should've seen the way
out of my living room interrogation.
I should've said "What girl
wears lipstick in kindergarten?
You know why I didn't kiss her back?
Because I have home training."
I should have made her into a Delilah.
If I mentioned Delilah, my mom
would've known I did listen
to the sermons while me and the other ushers
thumped each other or took turns
nodding on the back pew.
I wasn't old enough to think
of that, wasn't old enough to kiss a girl
and blame her for having lips.

Maybe Janus

Never really planned on being a god
of clumsy first date kisses,
annual reports, jamboree games,
jump balls, lead-off hitters (can you imagine
Henderson praying to anyone
but Henderson?), security
deposits, drug deals gone
good, Kindergarten romances, James
Meredith and Autherine Lucy and Crispus Attucks,
comic book reboots, budding
breasts in gym class—how many
throats have gushed
for the smallest
breeze or sprinkling?

What if he just wanted to work
on doors? What's he supposed to do
with a handful of keys
other than his best
Mr. Miracle impersonation
when you want him to catch
time by the tail and hold it
long enough for you to clear
your throat and spit
out a pretty girl's name?

Home Games

Every year, an old man takes me
for an undersized DB or running back

while we trade shots and histories. *What*
year did you play? You should have

played for us, We could have
used you tonight. So much melts

from their mouths
when I admit I haven't worn a uniform

since third grade and they see me
for what I am: a black man who learned

to shoot white liquor in a college town. Lust leaves
their voices. Hands leave my shoulders.

I spend the night paying
for my own drinks.

After I Heard Another White Woman at the Bar Talking About Michael Vick and the Death Penalty

Mike, I wanted to hit her
with a history lesson
about black men

never getting what they deserve
from the law.
But she'll go to OJ,

I'll go to Emmett Till,
She'll say I can't think
of what it's like to lose

a pet and I'll say
she can't understand because she doesn't
have a black dick between her legs

and America around her neck
and she'll say it's not the same
and that's the only thing we'll agree on

before her boyfriend shows up
with a shot and a shrug for everyone.
Thing is, Mike, I wanted to hit you, too,

years before the first shovel
touched your backyard
in Virginia. But it wasn't because of the rape

stands and electrocutions; it was because you ran
circles around my linebackers on *Madden 2004*.
You took away my safety

blitzes and zone coverages.
If you finished the game, I was finished,
so I hit you every play.

I hit you on run plays.
I hit you on pass plays.
I grinned every time

your virtual body broke
and my opponents turned into Priam
weeping over Hector's corpse

or some other Trojan father whose son caught
a spear with his throat.
They didn't want to go on without you

as their leader. The contest wasn't worth
the dollars on the coffee table
if you weren't standing.

They would swear they learned
to never gamble their future
on the shoulders of one man again.

It was nice to see the world care
about a black body so much,
even if I wanted to break it.

Fenrir's High School Reunion

Can't believe I shaved
for this shit, tried to

give a new face to the first people
who held my head

in their laps. Of course,
we only talked

about the Thor movie,
how much it hurt to watch Loki

tell jokes while the universe snapped
apart. But they say it's just

his character. They know him
better than I do. At least there's chicken

fingers. And there's a girl frowning
over at her mother's attempt

to explain how the world can have
chicken fingers even

if chickens don't have fingers.
The girl chooses an apple, and the adults

laugh because we remember our own
childish dogma, the things we swore

we would never put in our mouths.
All of the growling

bellies we made into gospel
choirs. It still smells like home

room. Hopeful bodies hugging
faithless bones. Pockets of sex. I miss

all of the pictures. I keep feeling
something stuck between my teeth.

Count Fenring

Never forget the miracles
that would've happened—

if the knee didn't snap senior year
if the fight didn't break out
if the transmission didn't go out
if the water heater didn't crack
if the alarm didn't turn off
if the boyfriend didn't pull out
if the cops didn't pull up
if the financial aid office would've answered the phone
if the post office acted right
if the roommate could've covered the shift
if the god mama prayed to was on time in this time zone—

It hurts to look
down and see the ones who should have been
standing on your throat, who used to leave you
begging for a call after crossing you up,
leave you writing poetry at the lunch table
after letting you down. The face
of a false future never moves
out of your memory, never grows dull
as a shinai. You never stop feeling
the breath in your ear, the hungry
toe at your heel.

When Your Favorite Rapper Makes a Comeback Album

Or makes his comeback
in a Cheerios commercial

or VH1 dating show,
you'll try to hide your anger.

He'll keep swearing
he's tired of the drugs and the gangs

of women in his Jacuzzi,
and you'll catch yourself believing him.

He'll wear a suit on his album cover,
and you will imagine all the little

boys in the mirror learning to tie a tie,
begging their moms for Stacy Adams

instead of Jordan's.
You dream of a bullet

meant for a black body left
cold in its chamber. A gun traded in

for grad school. You imagine
that maybe, maybe, there's a hole

in the rap game that you can fill
with that one decent freestyle

you pulled off in the 6th grade bathroom.
It was so slick it made all the boys forget they were high

fiving with their dicks out. You'll listen
to his newest album with time-stained

ears; you'll hear the notes
you missed the first thousand times

you hit "play" and let someone else
tell your girlfriend that you're sorry,

let someone else promise your mother
she'd never have to see you locked up again.

You'll really listen this time, and you'll hear
every reason why Diomedes didn't bother

with the Trojans in Italy, why Jim Brown
decided it was to time to run down

Hollywood drug dealers instead of running over
inside linebackers. You finish the rhymes

you never saw coming years ago;
you shrug your shoulders at the metaphors

that almost made you crash your car
on Campus Drive. You and your friends

will gather over the holidays for a wake.
You all ask your glasses why he didn't stop

sooner, why he didn't know it was time to quit.
On the way home, you'll dig for answers,

but then your beer-stained brain will go
to all the times you slid a desperate finger into the slit

of an arcade game's coin return searching
for one more life. All the times

you checked the mail
even when you knew you didn't have a chance

at the job. Every time you waved
at a future that was too busy texting to wave back.

You had to try one more time.
You already knew, but you had to know.

Native

Some black kid
had to be the first
black kid to taste white skin

in this neighborhood
and live, but I don't
know him. My granddad might've

lost a pool game to a bloody body
on Edmund Pettus.
My school was a battleground

when we played Ninja Turtles,
but that's all. I usually hear "nigger"
when someone asks "aren't you

tired of the word 'nigger'?"
What's it like? What's it like?
What's it like living

under a Rebel flag?
Sweat tea kisses? Lightning bugs?
We want to see our roots, make

sure we have some Indian in us
to explain the good hair and eyes dying
for dark liquor. But we can't track

John Henry's sweat in every subway.
We never talked about Rosa Parks
on the bus ride home. Everyone knew

men who could jump
in front of trains, women dying
to get off their feet.

RNC

Watch out for the “Knock Out
Game,” they tell us. They tell us it’s new;

they tell us it’s only one more
sign of how we don’t respect life,

but they don’t see us all
those summers ago, holding

our breath and clutching
our chests with our hands crossed—

like the pharaohs and mummies
we point to to prove black brains

existed before Wheatley—
while our friends push us

against the brick wall of our house
until we go black or exhale.

I could never black out;
I always gave up

the second my legs went light.
I don’t think about all the times I’ve struggled

for air until I see Eric Garner gag
in HD for the 2nd, 20th, 200th time,

and I still can’t help
but go back to being a kid

in the Peter Crump lunch line.
I stood proud of my clearance

rack Hilfiger shirt and jeans hanging low
enough for the principal to scowl

and high enough for my mom
to let me out of the house

until my best friend slipped
his arm around my neck from behind

and squeezed until my legs left me.
He laughed, claimed “That’s the best

way to take down big niggers
like you.” We settled

back in line before the teacher
made it to the back

to see what we were making
all the noise over. I couldn’t speak up

to tell her. Besides, it was taco salad day,
and my neck wasn’t worth spoiling that.

If I Meet the Buddha on the Road

I plan on killing him
because that's what the idiom says
to do, and I'm really good
at following orders. I guess,
then, I would be the Buddha
if being Buddha is like being
a wrestling champ: to be
the man, you have to beat the man.
And if I beat Buddha, I could be the man
all the boys and girls in Alabama look up to,
all the children with that lean and hungry
look I see when I get off
on exit 168. I'd have to learn to live
with my gut. I'd have to find
real smart things to say instead
of the fake smart things that got me through
too many keg parties and got me under
too few shirts. But if I'm the Buddha, I'm done

hunting for the Buddha.
I have to drop the spear
and shield and Wesley Snipes
elbow strikes. I have to hold my head high
and wait for a starving knife to lick my throat.
So Buddha, when I meet you on the road,
I'll keep my chin down and keep moving. And you,
you keep walking. Don't ask about the blood.
Don't ask about the blood on my hands,
and I won't ask about yours.

Now That Wally West Is Black

The next time he makes Superman
look like a Big 10 linebacker
in a bowl game, I'll have an "of course
the World's Fastest Man is black" joke
primed and ready. My nephew

will have one more action figure
I won't feel guilty about on Christmas.
I won't have to say Wally is kinda like
Iron Man, or he has a hammer, but not as cool
as Thor's. He'll be confused

by the *Justice League* cartoons.
He'll follow the alternate timelines
and alien doppelgangers without blinking,
but when the Flash slows down
enough to let the world catch him

winking his blue eyes,
the nephew will have questions,
and I'll have to promise him
that a Flash can be black,
just like a policemen, president, the first

pair of lips that taste
like lightning in our mouths.
And I'll tell him the Flash is only a red blur
most of the time, so his skin doesn't matter,
but we'll both know I'm lying.

Janus at Happy Hour

Ain’t nothing wrong with looking
back. You want to see

the first ass you grabbed
in the rearview, the first paychecks. The time

you stood in the mirror soaked in sex
and sophomore pride. Remember your broken

nose and paperless birthdays. No, brother,
going back ain’t the problem. I’d break my neck

to do it if I didn’t have an extra head
to do it anyway. Nah, forward

is the bitch; that’s some scary
shit. You never thought that homecoming

dance to Boyz II Men would be the only piece
of heaven you touch in this life. Dust and surgical

scars and bedroom apologies. Look at that lonely first
place trophy. Hell, man, boxers swear punches hurt

when you don’t see them coming. They don’t
know shit.

One Time for Woodley Park

I left, but I ain't never leaving Woodley Park.
Can't outrace the big bodies painted up like Skittles and John Deere.
Let's run it back one more time before it gets too dark.

Concrete Sugar Bowls in the summer split my knees like tree bark,
and I learned to keep my fists up whenever Ridgecrest boys were near.
I left, but I ain't never leaving. Woodley Park

was in my veins in undergrad every time a last call spark
drove me to whisper in a forbidden blonde's ear.
Let's run it back one more time. Before it gets too dark

the next day, she'd ask where I grew up, make a remark
about my vocabulary, and we wouldn't talk for a year.
I left, but I ain't never leaving Woodley Park.

Made it to college because mom and dad made me Clark
Kent, saved me from a doomed manual labor/minimum wage sphere.
Let's run it back one more time before it gets too dark.

Not even mad about the break-ins and black eyes—a shark
is a shark. No name on the bullets, so no use for fear.
I left, but I ain't never leaving Woodley Park.
Let's run it back one more time before it gets too dark.

Clark Kent's High School Reunion

Honestly, they don't remember him
wearing glasses, so he kills them

with a joke about the big city lights ruining his eyes.
They keep mentioning his dead dad,

keep asking how his dog is
still up and running

after all these years. That's all
he was: a boy with a dead dad

and a cool dog, so they fill the chasm
of lost days with baby pictures

and mental maps that can't place his home
on the right or the left of the new IHOP.

He has to pretend
he can't hear

the heartbeat of the fetus
when the couple

makes their announcement.
He has to pretend

he didn't watch
the finals of the state playoffs

from three worlds away.
He has to pretend

he's powerless
just like the rest of them

when the talk turns to the evil
Wal-Mart Supercenter and the unbreakable

Monsanto contracts.
He has to pretend

it was the whiskey that made him fly
to the bathroom to listen for catastrophes

under the cover of a stall, listening for the scream
of an idiot falling off the hotel roof

after too many shots of Jager and nostalgia.
But mostly, as always, he was watching

over Lois. He knew all
about what this town could do to outsiders.

For Tequila and All the Black Girls with Black Names

I keep the memory of our relationship alive
for laughs, for cheap

transitions when I hate myself
for sucking on another

lime that could have been
a loan payment, when I can taste

inertia on the rim
of a plastic cup.

Me and my friends for the night laugh
at what your mother must've been

thinking, kill ourselves
with a picture of where you must be now.

What could the world do with you:
a redbone girl from Montgomery

with a bad name?
We put you in the corner

office of a law firm, in the locker
room of a Tampa strip club.

But we never see your happy
hour moments when you beg

your friends to pull it together
while you riff on your 6th grade

boyfriend who wore white jeans
because of Bad Boy videos.

We don't see you earning
high fives for dating a poet

and teaching him how to kiss without opening
your wrists a decade later.

Back then, you and I promised each other
we'd be friends after the breakup

on Valentine's day. At least
one of us lied.

Vesta

When I ask you if you need me
to help in the kitchen, I don't plan on helping
you in the kitchen. I want to

make sure you see that I see you searching
for the cutting board in cabinets hiding
the dorm room pots we promised to replace

three years ago. I see you chewing
your nail and guessing if a plate is clean
enough for a Tuesday dinner. It's not

laziness that keeps me on the couch
or the uselessness of a last child
who never learned how to sweat

onions and garlic. It's religion, or all
the religion I kept after Montgomery
and sophomore lectures on Cybele

and the secret history of blood
sacrifices. Sometimes, I just need to see god
work and get out of the way.

Two-Face God

I know the Two Face God
is the god of my city
because the seal names us
the father of the Civil War and Civil Rights.
Black boys running
for Jefferson and Lee
on Friday nights. And then we all ran
when somebody thinks somebody saw a gun
in the stadium. We ran until the dogs
and police stopped us
from running. We ran until we ran
into the light-skinned girl we thought about when we flexed
our pudgy chests in the mirror.
We stopped running long enough to run
our mouths about how much we hoped
nobody stepped on our new Reeboks because we hoped
she noticed our new Reeboks because we knew she wouldn't
notice them at the after party because we lied
when we said we were going to the after party
because at midnight we'll be tiptoeing
to our bedroom and cursing
the Krystal's bag for crinkling and hoping
we don't wake up mom because it's Christmas
season and she has to clock in in three hours.

I know the Two Face God
is the god of my city
because I woke up
on my wedding day
in the same room

where I created my first childhood memory of swearing through my tears
that no one would ever love me.

I know the Two Face God
is the god of my city because the police
got so tired to coming to Montgomery
Mall that they put a police station in Montgomery Mall.

I know the Two Face God
is the god of my city because I can't help
but grin whenever somebody mentions the Confederates
failing after they moved to Richmond.

I know the Two Face God
is the god of my city because he is a god of nothing
but doors, a door to keeping
air force bases open and Southern eyes closed.
A door to keeping the west side on the west side
until damn near all of my city is the west side.

I know the Two Face God
is the god of my city because every prayer
we sing is a lie as big as the lie that makes us
believe in beginning or endings.
Show me a beginning
and we'll both stare into a black dying
to lick the color from our eyes.

I know the Two Face God
is the god of my city because my city is
not a cradle. It's a crater. Something big crashed
down here. Might have a been a chain
reaction of a million American dreams colliding.

Might have been the remains of a god ripped
to ribs and limbs by a mob of impossible prayers.

We Love Throwback Thursday

Because we get to believe history
is behind us, time is nothing

but a picture in a drawer
we can post on a wall and laugh at

with our friends. The hair cuts
and the cutoffs, braces and prom night

breakups. Let's pretend history doesn't hang
on our bodies like the black blood

and spear points and horse shit
and human shit on Hector's corpse.

Of course they burned the body,
but we can't burn our body

of work; our history's here: the scars
that meet us in the shower, our hairline,

credit line, line we won't cross
to touch a warm chest in the morning.

Lines move, but time doesn't
work in lines, doesn't work

like the interstate: exits passed
and forgotten, rest stops marked

miles beforehand. We draw time
machines in the margins

not because the past is out of our grasp
or because the future is a Sphinxian riddle.

We wish it took black magic
or a black hole to touch yesterday.

We wish most tomorrows weren't
as predictable as the sun.

Hacking

There's blood on the streets in Montgomery, and all of it
isn't on Jim Crow hands or dog teeth.
Blood from knees and elbows scraped white, from noses busted
by knees and elbows and no look passes
when no one was looking. I'm guilty and proud. I was the playground
Anthony Mason. My game wasn't pretty
enough to be Jordan or Olajuwon. I wasn't pretty.
All shoulders and menace, blocking
bodies or blocking shots made no difference.
I never hit a game-winner, but I did grab
12 rebounds in a pick-up game.
I counted my rebounds in pick-up games. I still do
not believe the stories waiting for me at home; friends swear
I gave birth to the scars they show off at the bar
during holiday meetups. I've never been in a fight
over money or a girl; I probably won't beat my kids unless
there's a Dairy Queen close by to help me
with my apology. But I butchered boys
to keep them from putting a ball through a net.
And other boys did nothing
but give me high fives.

Friday the 13th

He was my favorite monster. I was even cool
with the nightmares after the movies.
When I dreamt of being a freestyle rapper,
my name was Vorhees, and my finishing line
was going to be "it must be Friday
the 13th because Jason's killing
everybody," and then the DJ would stop
the beat and the crowd would unhinge
like Rucker after Durant dropped four straight 3s.
It wasn't just the name or the machete or the fear
of swimming, though; I wasn't just rooting for him
when he cut a teenager in two. I was pulling

for his mother, a mother willing to kill the rich
and lucky camp kids. What was Jason even doing
at that camp? Where was his letterman jacket,
Camaro, frisky girlfriend? Look at his clothes.
How much did his mom scrape
together to give him that vacation?
How many deals did she make
with landlords? How many times did she cut
the lights on and sigh? Could she afford a funeral?
At least the lake bed was free.

Campus

I lost my key—maybe god
took it—my first day here.

So many signs pointing
back to my twin

bed in Montgomery. Left-handed
desks in Latin class. Rats

behind the stove
we only touched to look for rats.

The phone on Friday night sitting still
as Persephone's spine

when the first golden leaf falls into her hair.
The looks from the future

housewives of Hoover
when I mentioned Persephone

around the keg. Lost
quarters in the dryer. Lost hours

looking for another black face
in Latin class.

How did my brother and sister survive
this place? How

many teeth did they leave behind
in the gravel parking lots

while they prayed to spirits
who never visited this part of town?

Wally West Attends Another Justice League Funeral

I've seen every punch this world will ever throw
and have seen this world punched out
of existence by the sun

eaters and savages. I've wiped the blood
of every hero from my mouth, tasted
their resurrection in my nose. But what good

is all the history of the world versus the questions
of a widow crying over her broken god?
Why him why now why not us why not me?

I have the answer, but one sermon is enough;
no one needs two voices
selling the values of the next life

to a crowd who's seen the heart
of stars and the edges of reality.
And what good would it do

to tell her, tell them all
that he's coming back? Would they rest
any easier if I told them every failure

they could have avoided, every ruin
they prevented in another version of this world?
If they knew they couldn't stop the bullet

aimed at their father's chest, would they stop
reaching for it? Would they smile in the mirror

if I told them they were the best version

of themselves the galaxy could manage?
If I told them to choose a thousand unborn
universes or the name tattooed on their wrists,

the names they hide under their cowls and bracelets
and capes? If I told them that on all the infinite earths,
this is the one only one where they'd have to cry

like this? They think standing still is murder
to me. Praise me for not shuffling my feet
off to another dimension. I wish I could

stand forever and count
the grains of dirt filling the grave. Can I
stay here?

Remix

Friends pass you a link,
tell you there's something

you need to hear, a video
you have to see. A few seconds

in and you recognize
the beat, recognize the hook

comes from a song your mom used
to hum in the kitchen while she waited

for the apple pie to cool.
And you turn it off, disappointed again,

tired of hearing the same song.
You know every myth

is a retelling, a sample
of the music that moved

your parents' hips, no matter
how hard it is to imagine

your folks grooving at Homecoming,
slow dancing with the lump

that will be your sister between them.
You know this song;

you don’t need to finish the first verse
to guess it begins with a black boy leaving

home too soon and ends with a father sad
for all the times he told the boy to stand up

and act like a man, a mother
begging to put her baby back in her body

instead of handing him over
to the earth.

Never Have I Ever

Most nights, we didn't know what we were drinking
for: shame or celebration. Were we
proud of pissing our pants
in the last five years, jerking off
to foreign language
teachers? Was it hubris or humility that made us
raise our beers? Or was it the blue
eyes across from us? The eyes grew
and glowed and narrowed
when we kissed the rim
of our cups. The eyes kept us company between
cigarette breaks. We're not listening
to the questions anymore.

Something about hands.
Something about razors.

The blue eyes look drunk
and need a ride home. The blue eyes make us
stay the night, but the blue eyes just fall
asleep on the couch. We're terrible
liars, and we whisper this to the blue eyes
the minute after they close.

Kobe vs. MJ

-For Terrance, Gary, Langston, and all the other brothers in the ring with me

The first time someone called me out
of my name and called me a

younger version of you, I was Pyrrhus flexing
in his father's armor, wearing the mean

grin only given to young boys the world can't stop
getting on its knees for. I saw the lightning leave

your eyes, dreamed of you as a dim Phoenix
in the corner talking shit about all the earth

you could crack open if you had a pair
of hands still blessed by the gods.

There would be no gods left when I was done
stepping over the walls even you couldn't climb.

But we know the cost of prayers
and the interest paid on their returns.

We, shiny stars, we know what sets the universe spinning
like a boy's ball on the first hopeful day of the new year.

We know the only thing the heavens need
more than gods is young bodies to feed

to the altars. I couldn't carry your shield; no one can
hear those words, though. Who cares

for the difference in the shade of black
on the edge of the scalpel or cleaver?

You're a surgeon, and I'm a butcher,
but what is blood other than blood?

Medea's High School Reunion

The girl with the magic
mouth, the mouth too good
to fit around the neighborhood

boys. The girl who put out
for the big city and left her family
in pieces over it.

The girl who left behind
rumors only the drunks and holy
would whisper about. The girl

no one really knew
how to greet when she floated
into the room dragging dragons

on a leash. The girl who laughed at light
beer and took a bottle of black
label to the corner before anyone could ask

how the kids were doing, why
didn't the husband make the trip.
The girl who won't give up her secrets

of why we can't see all the magic
it takes for her to raise
her head when someone calls her name.

An Apology to Montgomery

For every time
I checked my locks
when I got off on exit 170.

For every time
I took the bass out my speakers at a red light.

For every time
I passed the public library and didn't drop off a book
with a black face on the cover.

For every time
I couldn't remember how to get back
to my grandma's old house.

For every time
I thought I was too good
for my grandma's rice with ketchup in it.

For every time
I rolled my eyes at pastor Houston
for talking about hanging with MLK.

For every time
I should've kicked a girl
out of my apartment when she said
I didn't sound Southern.

For every time
I laughed at a joke about Alabama
State or Montgomery Mall.

For every time
I missed the Turkey Day Classic parade.

For every time
I listened to the gunshot
rumors at Cramton Bowl.

For every time
I pretend I'm more
than a coin flip
away from being another Alabama boy
on an airbrushed t-shirt.

Janus Bifrons

Imagine a second
throat behind the reflection, a tendril

hanging from your shadow and catching
on a secret

edge of the world.
The eyes for your enemy's widow,

the mouth that bites your lover's chest
and drips margarita salt into the wound.

Of course the gods have different names
in each city, a different hand

for the war horn or weathervane.
How many faces have you collected?

Who names you Guardian
of Hours? Wrecker of Dreams?

Scenic

I take the long way home so my wife can see where I ran
into a car during a summer game of street
football. I show her the house

where my friends marveled at the biggest
satellite we'd ever seen and wondered
how many scrambled bodies could pass

through a dish that size. I point
out the houses that held my Hectors
and Helens, yards that housed hellhounds who chased

us when the basketball went over the wrong fence.
It was a two man job. We found our real friends
when one of them grabbed us before we put a nervous hand

on the metal and said "I got the ball. You watch
the dog." She almost understands why we don't have a dog
yet when we pass JR's house and I have to mention

the murder. While we're quiet I lie
about trying to look him up because I never knew him
by anything but JR and nobody ever cared

about what JR really stood for.
Maybe he's a Jr. Maybe he's like me
and those are his initials.

We loved him, though, because we had to
love anybody in the neighborhood with a goal
in his yard and a sister who wasn't too good to wave

at sweaty dudes trying to act
like they weren't sweaty dudes
who didn't know how act around girls

who waved back. I'm letting the neighborhood down
just like I let my team down every time JR snuck by me
for an easy layup in a Malabar vs. The Rest

of Woodley Park game. I want to send him a copy
of my first book and write a note that says "This
is for the neighborhood,"

but he might have been thinking the same thing
when he shot up the school parking lot. The neighborhood
might be the last circle of hell he wants

to remember, the last reminder
he wants of when the only boundaries we imagined
were the size of a backyard.

My Kids

Won't ever amount to anything
other than hypotheticals. At steak

and wine dinners I can't afford, I'll wave
a tipsy hand and mumble "If

I had kids…" before the real parents beat you
back into a sober corner

of my mind. For you,
I'd love to snap

chin straps, learn
more than I ever wanted to know about Barbie

and her Ken vs. Steve love
triangle under your bed.

I could make room—beer
bottles for baby bottles. Even

then, you'd still be trapped
with me inside of you,

me making you vomit
in a college parking deck,

making you believe every "I love you"
is a Halloween

apple packed with razor blades. I bite
my tongue when the family gets hungry

for nephews and grandbabies to bounce
and pinch and play *Mario Kart* with.

You could be so much
better than me. And you could be

just like me. How
many times have you heard the world

tell me I'm just like my dad?
Have you seen my eyes?

They're not mine; Mom
gave them to me. So I'll see you

on the couch cushion between
me and the girlfriend. I'll keep you

inside. Swallow hard
like Saturn and hope

you never crawl
out of my throat.

Janus Works the Door

My universe is a sea
of Polo shirts and citrus
lotions brushing

my shoulders. Youth begging
to enter. Youth dying
to leave buried

in another's arms. I have never been a god
as much as I am now. The prayers
and promises and offers

grow fatter than red heifers.
Does a door ever matter
more than on a 21st birthday?

The faces never match. Who
am I to judge? I know the future
as well as you. Eyes shift

like my brethren locked in stars.
Once, I knew a man
who grew into a god by crossing over

a river and bedding a golden girl.
It's not hard to leave a face behind.
I sweep up dozens every night.

Thanksgiving

Growing up, I never saw any whites
only bathrooms, never had paper
bags pressed to my cheek. But
I had to find my dinner at the back door
of a hotel. I walked into a scene

from the kitchen of George Wallace's heaven—black
bodies stuffed in sterling coats, heads down, hands dancing
knives through onion and ox-tail.
The smell of a million missing fathers.
My father was somewhere

in that smell. And sometimes, his voice
would cut through the clatter,
sometimes another tired voice called me
over to a pan of chicken
or the type of meatballs hipsters blog about

these days. My knees buckled once or twice;
the pans were heavier than bone
and grease and sauce. My brother
kept the car running by the dumpster, left
the passenger's side open so I could slide in

and we could make our getaway.
We were back on the boulevard
before a manager had a chance to notice
a beat up Chevy on their lot,
before we had a chance to look back.

Trayvon's High School Reunion

We'll have to shoot
a last minute email
to the caterers to keep the Skittles
off the snack table. We'll bother

to leave out a jar for the Next Black Boy
to Breathe College Air Scholarship Fund.
We'll have a moment of silence for all
the dead bodies we forget to name.

We'll tell the DJ to scratch
over all the gunshot adlibs, leave
the Public Enemy in the crate.
We'll take a head count before every slow jam,

guarantee everyone has a shoulder
for their wet cheeks, a buffer
for every mumbled prayer god
will pretend to never hear.

Follow Through

In the summer, My father beat us
with 30-foot three-pointers
whenever he could

con me and my brother
into a backyard game.
I can still hear the ball hitting

the net with the sound of god slicing
a star on a cutting board.
It was one of the only moments

of finesse we had in a house of fried
bologna and cracked mirrors.
He should have pushed

his shoulder into our hairless chests
and bullied his way to the basket,
bruised us into being men

because Montgomery leaves bruises
on all of her children. He could've let us
grow into our scraped knees, bounced

our heads on the concrete a couple of times.
We were honor roll kids; we would've been
fine. He could've been harder on us,

shown us a shadow
of the man we saw when he told us
to throw a stick in the spokes

of any boy in school who fucked
with us and tried to ride away,
the shadow of the man who did a tour in Jim Crow

Alabama and Base X. We never saw that man;
we only saw the ball
arcing through the hours of the day

and his small smile when we begged
for one more game, one more chance
to try to reach an inch higher than his fingertips.

Household Gods

I never live up to my vows
to get WD-40 for the doors.

Every morning, the hinges call me
a liar. How many lies are caught

in the squeal of a dying door? The screws
will forget their purpose soon.

The world beneath us is sliding or breaking
or dead already and we are busy

arguing over what
is the best way to separate mythology and history

on the bookshelf. No matter
how many times we move

the TV or argue over the coffee table,
this home is nothing

but a door and fire
somewhere behind that door.

It's practical, like concrete,
arches, aqueducts, roads

lined with corpses rotting on crosses.
A door and a fire. Janus

and Vesta: a loyal woman
and a two-faced man giving

one set of teeth to compliment the lasagna
and another to ward off the solicitors.

This home is either the start
or end of civilization. Home takes me

forward and backward, so I am a god
of our doorway, but I'm also a dog.

Part ouroboros, part German shepherd
chewing its tail.

I only stop spinning to snarl
whenever I smell a wolf

in the yard, whenever I hear curious hands pawing
at the lock, whenever I sense

a piece of my past getting close
enough for you to see it.

Alabama, 2013

The state pays me
to teach proper English
to future governors

and mistresses.
I have a book in a glass case
next to Ovid and Gibbon

in the Classics building.
The students who bother to look
up probably think I'm white,

dead, and important. Am I
feeling what Alexander felt
when he put Asia under his boot,

when he avenged Athens
and the 300 Spartans? This is victory:
my name on a door, the descendants

of George Wallace blushing when I call them
articulate and avoiding my eyes.
But Alexander never lived

through the agoge, and the cops here
let me drive home drunk
with the same warning they give everyone else.

Some of my ancestors would look up to me
as a god, the son of Deliberate Speed
and We Shall Overcome. Some of them would

look down and wonder
how I can stand on their graves
and still end up so short.

When Your *Madden* Running Back Retires

You curse him,
shrug, note

his speed dropping
two points a season

for the last
three seasons,

relive the fumble
in the January snow,

relive the shoulder injury
that kept you from going

undefeated. You never needed
him. But you wanted

one more 1,000 yard year,
one more run

with the gem
you discovered in the muck

of a fifth-round video game draft.
You want him to last

a little longer because
if his knees have finally gone,

you have to think about your knees
and the songs they sing

when you trade one can for another
in the kitchen. He's gone

away to spend more time with his family.
When was the last time you called your family?

You do remember that it was family
that put the controller in your hand

in the first place, don't you?
The envy only second sons can know

pushed you to push buttons faster,
to push "mute" so mom didn't find

your hands pawing a wet
controller in the dead of the night.

Your brother stopped beating you
years ago. Your mom's just happy

you're not dead and you're not asking
for money that much these days.

Your running back moved on.
Your video game grew up.

What happened to you? Really,
I'm asking.

Of Course We Lost the War

Gates and the temple
dedicated to giving the world time
to sharpen its blade
for battle or a welcome home buffet.
You'd think it was important enough
to memorialize or preserve. You can
almost see some Vandal
or Gaul or Goth tapping a haggard Roman
on the shoulder
and vowing to leave the temple alone
while he loaded his arms with gold
and girls. Some Dark Age
carpenter picking through the bones
of the eternal city would leave
the stones behind, leave a note
behind for history.
But, in every age, a gate is only

a gate. And, sometimes, a closed gate
is scarier than an open gate
because—when all the locks
in the world click shut
and the sentries slump
and no one needs
a new missile or shield—

who can explain
why your dreams still end
in blood choking your last prayer
or your teeth breaking like light

bulbs when you eat your next birthday
cake? Where is the god
who can tell you why
peace still sounds like Aeneas
searching for the name of a dead friend?

My First Poetry Reading

Would have been my last
if my parents had their way.
My finale was a rhyming
quattrain about wanting

to get laid. The freshmen blushed
and the seniors backed me
up with whistles and claps. Of course,
my parents were upset. Thankfully,

they never unpacked
that anger in the car
ride home; they never did
show me what to do

with a balled fist
or a growl lost
in the echo of cans
rattling in a trashcan.

I never learned if the silence
hugging my chest tighter than the seatbelt
was born from their son
talking about sex

at sixteen when sex
at sixteen led to my first
sister who led to another sister
who led a brother who led to me.

Or the silence could have been shame
over a son who was better at writing poems
about getting laid than actually getting laid.
But they were children of Motown

lust and gospel choir confessions,
so they could have been mad for no reason
other than creating a son
who dropped wack rhymes.

Roll Call for Michael Brown

It will happen,
an honest mistake
in a hot August classroom.

Someone will blink
at the name and swear *this*
"Michael Brown" can't be

that "Michael Brown." Or Someone
will be too busy with her head down
finishing syllabi to look up and see the flash

grenades and tear
gas. Someone will be running
late, his mind on the cops

that will probably ticket him
for not having a permit.
Someone won't see why a name

is such a big deal. Someone will
read his name like the next item on a list
of groceries and move to the next student

before the first groan rumbles
through the stale Missouri air.
Someone will start to speak

his name and then cover his mouth
like a Roman priest closing Janus' door

and praying all the violence of the world will stop

short of his porch. Someone will ask,
"Michael Brown? Is Michael Brown here?"
and we will all have to answer.

January

Does it feel like the beginning
of something new? Yesterday stale in your mouth,

morning breath of car bombs and platitudes.
But the world is still

dying: another inch of snow and another inch
of waistline. And you thought you could leave

this behind because you tore a calendar
off your wall, because you were brave enough

to look at a phone number
and press "delete." Step outside. Step on

the scales. Do butterflies own this world?
Is that a new face you see in the microwave door?

This is the season of the two-faced god.
Don't believe his promises. Don't

let him palm your dreams
like a trick coin.

If All the Masters of Time Were My Slaves

They would give me a way out
of heritage,
not hate letters

to the editor.
Give me a lane
of interstate

that will take me past the stars
and bars on exit 200,
past Jupiter

Inn and the bodies
of all the broken
Impalas.

Give me a voice
the ladies in the checkout lane
can't resist

placing on a military base
or *Cosby Show* suburb.
Give me a brain big enough for all

of Caesar's subjects
and verbs and war tallies.
Give me the keys I need to turn every lock

into dust. And I would
still take King-Lee holidays,
dead church girls, boll

weevil shrines and Iron
Bowl prayers, every
extra syllable Southern girls add

to my name after the third Jim Beam.
I will take this home
because where else could be

home when my first name is Greek,
my last name is Gaelic,
and the world can't decide

if it's okay to call me negro,
colored, or just plain black,
non-Hispanic?

I will take the magic of a Montgomery Thanksgiving
filled with two rounds of pound cake
and my father asking about the State

game and my mother sighing
"I love you" before she gets ready
for black Friday at J. C. Penney

because my mother knows exactly one word
for love and I can only really hear it
when the air turns to syrup in the summer

and I'm at the table listening to a sermon
on Alabama sin delivered by a missionary
from the Colorblind North or the sons

of California who never claim
the blood of Watts, King, or Kennedy.
I will take every theory on time and space and black

Athenas and black Atlantics
and black holes as long as it leads
me back to Woodley Park.

Jason McCall is the author of *Silver* (Main Street Rag), *I Can Explain* (Finishing Line Press), *Dear Hero*, (Winner of the 2012 Marsh Hawk Press Poetry Prize) *Mother, Less Child* (co-Winner of the 2013 Paper Nautilus Vella Chapbook Prize), and *Two-Face God* (WordTech Editions). He is also the co-editor of *It Was Written: Poetry Inspired by Hip-Hop*. He holds an MFA from the University of Miami, and he currently teaches at the University of North Alabama.

Author website: http://jasonmccall.weebly.com

Press website: https://www.wordtechweb.com

Also by Jason McCall

Silver

I Can Explain

Dear Hero,

Mother, Less Child

Praise for Jason McCall

"Jason McCall's *Two-Face God* is not an easy read. It's a book that confronts hard truths about being black and male in the United States, a nation never ready for these confessions, these memories, these confrontations. It is, however, a fierce book, one that sits in its truths, one that demands your attention as it parses realities of black male life into a comic book mirror, invoking those childhood heroics to get this book's hero over, around, and under all the damage this nation puts on his very human shoulders. In the end, poetry is what saves this speaker, and we are gifted with his words, his legacy, his life."
— Allison Joseph

"Jason McCall's remarkable third collection *Two-Face God* is a modern-day reckoning with both of Janus's faces. These poems are full of the beginnings and transitions of doubt and disbelief—in our educations and institutions, in the various gods of applause and bedroom posters, in our youth and stubborn want to pretend we have a say in when it leaves. These deft and always sonorous poems create a new, American mythology, one that exists on the other side of double ply racial masks and the archways to segregated cities. And when the speaker of 'When Your *Madden* Running Back Retires,' says, 'Your video game grew up. / What happened to you?' we are left in our evolutions, looking for the answers we really don't want to find."
— Adrian Matejka

"Janus from the ruins of Rome, Wally West from the pages of DC comics, Count Fenring from the shifting sands of Dune… Again and again in Jason McCall's new book, we are confronted with the masked and doubled voices of outsiders, haunted and hungry souls who feel like fakers in their own skin, perhaps traitors, perhaps unsung heroes who no one could possibly believe in. From the linoleum halls of his Montgomery high school to the marble halls of Vahalla and Justice,

Jason McCall's various voices serve as aegis between a real boy who is gifted with great insight and the society/self that cannot fully embrace the exceptional. This book, a book about exclusion and acceptance, explores the experience of otherness from the perspective of the hero who, himself, is perhaps just as critical as the crowds that jeer when the speedster who wasn't supposed to win actually crosses the finish line first. Here we find a voice 'searching for one more life,' for a world where 'skin doesn't matter,' for a universe where God will just 'get out of the way,' for a life where the underdog who understands both past and future, both Telemachus and Trayvon Martin, Armageddon and Alabama, Woodley Park and Wally West cannot, will not, become the ultimate enemy."— Bryan Dietrich

Author photo: David A. Smith
Cover image: Pixabay.com

CPSIA information can be obtained
at www.ICGtesting.com
Printed in the USA
LVOW03s1704190318
570341LV00004B/919/P